The Birds and the Bees

The Birds and the Bees

How to talk to your young child about bodies, birth and sex

Genelle Gordon

DOUBLEDAY
SYDNEY•AUCKLAND•TORONTO•NEW YORK•LONDON

THE BIRDS AND THE BEES
A DOUBLEDAY BOOK

First published in Australia and New Zealand in 2002
by Doubleday

National Library of Australia
Cataloguing-in-Publication Entry

Gordon, Genelle.
The birds and the bees: how to talk to your young child about bodies,
birth and sex.
ISBN 1 86471 062 4.
1. Sex instruction for children. 2. Parenting. 3. Human
reproduction – Juvenile literature. I. Title.

372.372

Transworld Publishers,
a division of Random House Australia Pty Ltd
20 Alfred Street, Milsons Point, NSW 2061
http://www.randomhouse.com.au

Random House New Zealand Limited
18 Poland Road, Glenfield, Auckland

Transworld Publishers,
a division of The Random House Group Ltd
61-63 Uxbridge Road, Ealing, London W5 5SA

Random House Inc
1540 Broadway, New York, New York 10036

Cover photograph by Photolibrary.com
Illustrations by Deborah Clarke
Text designed and typeset in 12/17 Garamond Book by Midland Typesetters,
Maryborough, Victoria
Printed and bound by Griffin Press, Netley, South Australia

10 9 8 7 6 5 4 3 2

Contents

*To our children, who so lovingly teach us
how to be parents. And especially to Joshua,
Jacob and Hannah*

Preface

In today's rapidly changing society, and what can appear to be a sexually confusing world, it's hard for parents to know what to tell young children about bodies, birth, sex and sexuality. And in my years as an educator and counsellor on sexuality issues I have met many parents concerned about sexual abuse and the vulnerability of their children – parents who want to teach safety without frightening their children. Many parents know they want their children to be better informed than they themselves were about sexuality at the same age, but are just not sure where and when to begin.

I hope this book will encourage parents to be open and honest with their children and to feel more confident about their parenting when it comes to issues of sexuality, in order that we may bring up sexually healthy children.

I hope it can answer your questions, give an opportunity to open up discussion with partners, family and friends and also provide a chance to laugh at some of the more amusing aspects of children's sexual development as they come to terms with their body, its functions and the language used to describe them.

I have tried to use language that is inclusive of all the shapes and forms of family and of us as parents whether we are parenting alone, in pairs, or in a wider support system. The term 'health professional' in this book can be applied to whichever professional you turn to (for example, GP, midwife, naturopath, etc).

Happy parenting!

1

Where do you begin?

Knowing your own values

Some parents decide even before conception how they want to bring up their children on subjects such as education and attitudes to violence and racism. It's a good idea to be clear, too, about the kind of messages you want your children to receive about gender, sex and sexuality, and body issues.

I use the term 'sexuality' in its broadest sense. Perhaps one definition is that sexuality is about being male or female, and the roles of each, and how we relate to one another – it also includes the sexual behaviours but is not exclusively about sexual behaviours.

The Birds and the Bees

Do you want your child to use family terms for their genitals or do you want them to use clinical/medical terms? Are you going to bathe with the kids, and if so, when do you decide they are 'too old' for that? And how are you going to handle it when your two-year-old wants to touch your genitals in the bath? You might think that there is no need to discuss issues like these with your partner and family – after all, you think alike on so many issues, right? But our values are shaped largely by the way we ourselves were brought up as well as by our own experiences, and every family is different. How would you feel if your three-year-old son was playing with his penis in the bath and your partner told him he shouldn't or he'll go blind. Or if you heard your aging mother say to your four-year-old daughter that she needs to lose weight or she'll be a 'fat' girl and no one will want to marry her! And as relaxed as you may think you are about all this 'sex' stuff, it can be a real shock the first time a friend tells you that your child and theirs have been playing 'doctors and nurses'.

These are all 'sexuality issues' that you and your partner need to agree on if you are parenting as a couple, so that you can be consistent with your child and therefore provide an environment that is not too confusing for them. So talk to each other! If you are parenting alone, talk to friends, family or whoever is supporting you in your parenting role. Think about what messages you do and do not want to give your child. A fun way to begin this process is to sit down with a partner or friend and write down your answers to the following questions. Then share them with each other.

1. What is your first memory of the whole subject of sex and sexuality?
2. What or who was the biggest influence on your ideas?
3. When do you remember first seeing an adult naked, and what was your reaction?
4. What was the funniest misconception you held about sex?
5. Who could you talk to about these things as you grew up?
6. What significant messages did you receive from your parents about your gender?
7. How do you want your child to feel about their body and their gender?

This exercise helps us to clarify our values and beliefs, and where these came from. What you have grown up believing is valid and important – your children are going to learn a lot about sexuality from you. And this will happen regardless of whether you talk openly about it. Even though you've decided that you want your children to have more inform-ation than you had, your own long-established value system will dictate how comfortable you are with particular aspects of sexuality. Remember that chil-dren are like little sponges and just as they imitate you doing the dishes, shaving or putting videos in the VCR, they will imitate your way of relating to your partner and other people. They will feel your comfort or discomfort with bodies, your ease or unease with words that describe the body and they will do as you do. But if for example you are uncom-fortable with nudity, you don't have to force your-self to cartwheel across the living room naked! Be honest with yourself and your child; it seems to work best. If they ask you why it's not okay to run around the house naked when Sam Smith's family go swimming in the nude, explain that you feel embarrassed being naked in front of other people or seeing them naked and in this family you all keep your clothes on except in private. See Chapter 4 for more about answering children's questions.

Gender identity

'Gender is the single most important aspect of our personal identity. We cannot think of ourselves without being aware that we are male or female.'

Stevi Jackson, author
Childhood and Sexuality

Messages about gender are powerful and we pass most of them on to our children unconsciously. By the age of three, children have a fairly clear sense of what sex they are and many of the expected behaviours of that sex (the gender roles). This is when you hear your little boy saying things like he wouldn't want that toy because it's a 'girl's thing' and vice versa. If you have made every effort to be a gender-conscious parent and have introduced your child to 'equal' opportunities it can be dismaying to see the genetics of sexual identity versus the learning of gender identity come into play. The old nurture versus nature debate seems never-ending. But in reality children learn much of this boy–girl behaviour simply by watching the males and females around them.

If you say that boys should be allowed to express their feelings, but then comfort your four-year-old son with 'You're a big boy now, don't cry', he learns to repress, not express, those feelings of sadness or hurt. If you praise your daughter for always looking pretty and helping others, but seldom comment on her intellectual ability, she learns that looking pretty and caregiving are her gender's key roles. This is not to say that either is a good or bad message, but it is important to know you are giving messages like these every day to your child. Research tells us that we do treat the genders differently: that boys stop being given affection by their parents much earlier than girls, and that girls are still principally encouraged to think of others' feelings before they think of their own.

Gender equity for males and females is much more than just the opportunity to play with trucks, dolls houses, kitchens and tools. It is about valuing the differences between the genders and acknowledging that each has special qualities, which need to be given equal importance within society and within relationships between men and women. Equity is more about the acknowledgment of differing strengths and talents, than expecting boys and girls and men and women, to be the same as one another.

Some parents become concerned when their little boy wants to play with dolls and his best friends are girls. This concern is about sexual orientation and a misguided fear that the child will 'become' gay. Have you ever noticed that we seldom put as much effort into discouraging girls from climbing trees or playing with trucks, as we put into discouraging boys from 'feminine' pursuits such as dressing up and wearing jewellery? This is part of our socially ingrained fear of gay people (homophobia) and there is more about this in Chapter 5.

Girl: Let's dress in this dress.
Boy: I'm not allowed.
Girl: Yes you are, just put it on.
Boy: My dad said I'm not allowed to. He said I'm a sissy.
Girl: No you're not. You're a boy!

Two children observed at a Playcentre, from New Zealand Playcentre Magazine, *October 1995*

So be aware of the messages you convey to your kids – sexuality is very much about gender and gender is very much about sexuality.

As a child moves from infancy to early childhood to adolescence, their interactions with others and the decisions they make are inextricably linked to them being male or female, boy or girl, woman or man. To look at those wider issues more closely I recommend you read parenting books that focus on raising boys or girls, such as *Raising Boys* by Steve Biddulph or *Parenting Girls* by Susanna De Vries and Susan Stratigos Wilson. These books are intrinsically about sexuality and gender issues.

2

First
anatomy
lessons

The genitals

It can be difficult to talk about bodies if you're not too sure yourself which bits do what, or if you don't know all the clinical terms, so this chapter aims to clear up some of the mystery.

Girls

Girls are born with all their ova (eggs) inside them, around about 300 000 of them. These eggs sit inside the ovaries until puberty, which is when they start to mature and 'ripen'. One will then be released each month, which will usually result in menstruation (a period). So your little girl has a womb, ovaries and eggs right from pre-birth. She also has a clitoris but this has no function in reproduction.

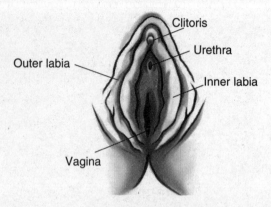

The female genitals

It is a very sensitive area, which gives pleasure to most women when touched. If there had been a Y instead of an X chromosome at conception, your little girl's clitoris would have turned into a penis about four months after conception.

Caring for girls: While she's an infant the anal (backside) and vulval area (where the vagina and clitoris are) need to be cleaned at every nappy change to prevent rashes.

From around age three she can wash this area herself with your encouragement. There is no need to use lots of soap on this part of the body as it can affect the delicate balance of tissue and fluid, especially within the vagina. Take it easy and use small amounts of mild soap.

It is not uncommon for little girls to develop thrush. Thrush is a fungal infection, which can lead to a red, raw and itchy vulval area. Discourage your child from scratching the area, as this will make it feel worse, and attend to it as soon as you can. Ask your health professional about what to use, and use any product only as directed. Anti-fungal creams can be bought at the chemist. Nappy rash creams, which contain zinc, may aggravate the condition so don't use them to treat thrush.

From around three years of age, children will be able to apply cream themselves if encouraged by you, if you are uncomfortable about touching their genitals. From four years onwards there really is no reason for any adult to be doing it, unless the child seems unable to.

When your daughter is learning to use the toilet it's a good idea to teach her to wipe from the front to the back (urethra to anus), so that bacteria are not brought forward from the anus into the vagina or urethra (pee hole).

If your daughter complains of pain when she urinates this may be a symptom of a urinary tract infection (UTI). Increase the amount of water she drinks and take her to your health professional. UTIs do need to be treated, and repeated infections would be a cause of concern.

If you notice any sores, blisters, rashes, blood or swelling, or your child complains of soreness or pain in the genital area, always have it checked out by a professional.

Boys

Baby boys aren't born with sperm, although their testicles (balls) are there and will further descend (drop down) once they reach puberty. This is when your son's testicles start to make sperm, which can

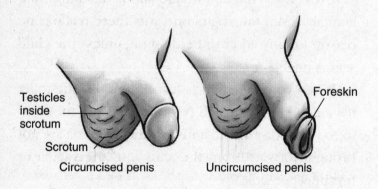

Testicles
inside
scrotum

Scrotum

Circumcised penis

Foreskin

Uncircumcised penis

The male genitals

fertilise a female egg. Your midwife or other health professional will check that the testicles have dropped a little when your son is only a few days old. Prior to birth, in the early months of your pregnancy, the baby developed either a clitoris or a penis from the same piece of tissue; with your little boy, it was a penis.

Boys can have erections from as young as a few weeks old. This is perfectly normal and is not about 'sex'; it has to do with the blood supply, warmth, a full bladder, and the sensations he is experiencing.

Caring for boys: Boys need to have their genital and anal area cleaned every day and in infancy this needs to be at every nappy change to avoid nappy rash.

From three years onwards they can be taught how to clean this area themselves, and teaching by showing how you do it is a good idea (if you're willing). There is no need to use lots of soap as it can be drying on the skin and many small children have very sensitive skin.

It is uncommon now for boys to be circumcised, except on the grounds of religion or medical necessity. So your little boy is likely to have a foreskin.

There is no need to pull the foreskin back to clean the penis and in fact you should not do this as it may cause pain or swelling. As the child grows and begins exploring his own body, he may start to pull the foreskin back himself from about the age of three or four years. You can encourage him to clean under his foreskin at that stage of his development. If you are a dad or male caregiver, you may be willing to show him how you clean under your own foreskin.

Sometimes the end of your boy's penis may look a little inflamed or infected. Dissolving a tablespoon of salt in his bath water can help clear this up. If the end of his penis is persistently inflamed and/or your child complains that it is sore, take him to see your health professional.

Little boys can get balanitis. Like thrush, this is a fungal infection and can be red, raw and itchy. Try to discourage your child from scratching the area and ask a health professional for advice. Anti-fungal creams usually clear it up quickly and some can be bought over the counter of your pharmacy. Nappy rash creams containing zinc only aggravate fungal infections.

If your son says that it hurts when he urinates

this may be a symptom of a urinary tract infection (UTI), so increase his water intake and seek advice from a professional. UTIs need to be treated.

If you notice any sores, blisters, rashes, blood or swelling, or your child complains of soreness in the genital area, always have it checked out by a health professional – it could be something that needs to be treated.

Naming the parts

If you are not comfortable using the clinical terms for the genitals you might like to start using the language before your child can talk. That way you can hope to become more at ease with saying the words out loud and they can learn them as part of their growing vocabulary. Just as you help children identify and name their nose, eyes, mouth and toes when you bath them or bathe with them, it's a good idea to name their buttocks, penis or vagina/vulva. You do not have to use clinical terms (such as vagina) in daily life if you really don't want to; in most families there are odd little words used for the genitals, such as 'fanny', 'diddle', 'willy' or 'tootsy',

Clinical term	Some family terms
Penis	Willy, diddle
Testicles	Balls, goolies, knackers
Scrotum	Sack
Breasts	Boobs, bosom
Vagina or vulval area	Fanny, tootsy
Buttocks and/or anus	Bum, bottom

and there is no harm in using those terms. However it is advisable to teach children the clinical terms as well, so if they ever need to tell a health professional, teacher or other adult about some pain or incident that involves their genitals, they can use language that will be understood by other people. After all, a 'tootsy' could be almost anything . . . including a Dustin Hoffman movie.

'My son came home from childcare very distressed one day. When I asked what was wrong he cried "It's not fair, Mum. All the other boys have got diddles and I've only got a penis!"'

Nicola, mother of a three-year-old

If your child asks at a later stage why there are two names you can explain that some people are comfortable with some terms and some with other terms – or that one word you use within the family and the other you use at the doctor's.

Touching and exploring

Around the time that children are being taught how to use the potty or toilet (from about two to three years of age) there is a lot of focus on their genital area, so this is a time when they are likely to start taking more notice as well. After all, you are watching and waiting for them to piddle or do 'number twos' and they are just as excited about the whole event when they get praised for having done it in the right place, don't be surprised if they then want to talk about it or touch it as well.

Just as your child learns about gender identity by observing how males and females act, they also learn about the differences of the sexes by noticing the obvious physical differences.

From very early on they may try to touch your genitals and breasts in the bath or if they see you naked. Children are very curious about their world and this includes your bits and pieces that dangle, wobble and have prickly hair growing all around.

> 'Mummy's got hedgehogs on her vagina.'
> *Joe, aged 2¹/₂*

It is really up to you how comfortable you are with your child's exploration of these areas on your body. As a rough guide, at around two to three years of age you may want to start introducing your child to the concept of genitals being 'special' or 'private' parts of the body that we don't let just anyone touch or look at. Let them know that we can tell people not to look at or touch our genitals when we don't want them to. This is also information that can help prevent sexual abuse (see also Chapter 5).

> 'My partner was standing at the sink in his short bathrobe one morning and our 18-month-old daughter went between his legs, grabbed his dangling penis and gave it a good strong tug!'
> *Marilyn, mother of a six-year-old*

Avoid using scary or shaming language, such as 'That's dirty, don't touch it' or 'Don't look at that, you're being rude'. Rather, explain *why* they should not touch or look.

The child's own sense of privacy will develop over the next few years, and there is no harm in introducing the concepts of privacy and safety from early on.

Children's desire to see and touch your genitals is very innocent, but don't be afraid to set limits about touching other people's genitals because if you don't teach what the limits are your child will not know.

'I was blowing raspberries on my two-year-old son's tummy after a bath and he said "Mummy blow penis too", and I thought, "Oh God! What do I say to that!."'

Jenny, talking about an experience with her first child

3

Playing doctors and nurses

Childhood sexual play

Sex play between children is normal and natural. They are curious little creatures and, just as they wanted to touch your genitals when they were bathing with you, they will want to check out their peers just to make sure they are made of the same stuff. They may also be curious about faeces and urine and wonder if things come out of those holes, can other things go into them?

Don't confuse this natural curiosity with something sinister, or worry that you have told them too much (see Chapter 4). All this activity is about discovery and is sensual – of the senses – rather than sexual in nature. By this I mean that their early childhood sexual play does not carry the sexual connotations of adult genital activity – remember, they are not adults and their actions are motivated by very different things. They are busy working out how they fit into the world, who they are like and who they differ from – it is all part of normal human development.

So what do you do if you discover your child with a playmate and they're displaying their genitals to each other? Firstly, don't panic! They'll possibly be just as surprised as you will at being caught, because most children learn very early on that sexual play somehow needs to be a private or secretive thing. How you react will have an impact on whether or not the child starts to feel shame about things sexual. Shame is not a healthy emotion; it is a feeling that equates to 'I am no good' rather than a feeling of 'I did something wrong'. You may of course be a parent who is very comfortable with the whole issue of childhood sex play and at ease with their exploration. But if you do not want the children to continue to play this game, suggest it's time to play something else; if you can acknowledge what they are doing and then ask them to move onto some other activity, all the better. For example, you could try simply saying, 'I can see you're curious about each other's bodies. Do you want to ask me anything? I might know the answer'. Answer their questions, then move them on to another game.

If you are really uncomfortable with the situation and do not want your child to participate in sexual play at all, then you need to explain that you don't like them playing that game and move them on to another activity. If they ask why you don't like it, tell them the truth about what you are uncomfortable with. For children to gain an understanding of your values they need to know a little about why you believe what you do, and that way they may begin to value it too. Again you may want to talk about privacy and who we allow to touch our genitals.

It is not helpful to become enraged and reprimand or threaten the children. Telling them that they'll go to prison, their genitals will drop off, or they'll go blind is cruel, and it's untrue. There is no need to exaggerate the consequences of their actions; usually they'll already be feeling a bit embarrassed.

Shaming, reprimanding and punishing children usually has the effect of pushing the activity 'underground' and can lead to secretiveness about sex and sexuality. It also tells the child you are not approachable on these issues and they will take their questions or concerns elsewhere.

If you think the games they are engaging in might cause actual physical harm then you need to point this out too, so they learn that objects don't get placed in the vagina or anus. These are delicate parts of our body and need to be treated gently. This could be a time to explain more about the functions of their genitals.

This kind of play between peers is normal and natural, whether they are of different sexes or the same sex – boys playing with boys or girls with girls does not indicate sexual orientation (in other words whether they are gay or not).

As long as there is no coercion and the children are similar in age, it is simply an explorative game. If there is more than a couple of years difference in ages, coercion may be involved or sex games dominate play and they aren't interested in much else, then you may need to look into the situation further. Listen to your child if they tell you that one of their friends is trying to get them to engage in such games when they don't want to, and it would be of concern if the children were engaging in activities that are decidedly adult in nature, such as simulating oral sex or using very sexualised language (not just the usual 'dirty' words). Don't jump to any immediate assumptions about sexual abuse, but look at the overall picture of the child's behaviour. If you see several things that worry you it would be wise to discuss your concerns with someone you trust who is knowledgable about child sexual abuse.

What's normal?

The range of what is considered 'normal' sexual behaviours in preschool children are:

- Touches, rubs own genitals when nappies/pants are being changed, when tired, going to sleep, tense, excited or afraid.
- Explores differences and similarities between males and females, boy and girls.
- Touches the genitals, breasts of familiar adults and children.
- Asks questions about genitals, breasts, intercourse, babies.
- Has erections (male).

- Likes to be nude. May show others his/her genitals.
- Interested in watching other people doing bathroom and toilet functions.
- Interested in how babies are born (both male and female).
- Uses 'dirty' words for bathroom and sexual functions.
- Interested in faeces/urine.
- Plays doctor/nurse inspecting others' bodies.
- Puts something in the genitals or rectum of self or other due to curiosity or exploration (no coercion/force involved).
- Plays 'house' – may simulate both male and female roles.

Adapted from 'Behaviours Related to Sex and Sexuality in Preschool Children', *Toni Cavanagh-Johnson, PhD, California 1994.*

The stages of sexual development that take place up to about age five are:

- Developing a sense of gender identity (their own sense of being male or female).
- Develops gender role (ideas of how males and females behave in society).

Playing doctors and nurses

- Has sensual feelings; erections (penile/clitoral).
- Finds genitals and masturbates.
- Learns to value self through nurturing body contact from others.
- Develops many important attitudes about sex from parents and other adults – models adult behaviours.
- Learns the language for genitals and body functions.
- Receives many unspoken messages from parents and other caregivers.
- Develops sense of what is considered acceptable behaviour limits, privacy and manners.
- Is curious about where babies come from, how they are made.
- Explores sexuality through play with dolls and peers.
- Is curious about differences/similarities in boys' and girls' bodies.
- Explores adult relationships by playing at being adult male or female.
- Is able to learn to say 'No' to unwanted touch.

A worksheet 'Stages of Sexual Development' for Bodies, Birth and Babies, *Peggy Brick et al. USA, 1989*

Masturbation

Masturbation is a natural activity. Infants usually start to find their genitals at around six to nine months old and may touch their genitals periodically from then onwards.

Some children begin to become really interested in their genitals at about two to three years old when they are learning to use the potty or toilet. It's as though the whole household is now focusing on their little genitals, so why not join in the party. 'Poos' and 'wees' can become big words in the vocabulary. If you react calmly to these types of words your child will tire of them quickly and move on, but if you become angry or upset they may keep saying them in order to provoke. They may also be curious about the feel of the urine and faeces, so don't be too distressed if they have a bit of a play with it once or twice.

As the child registers that their genitals have these interesting functions and they can control to some extent the 'on and off' switch, they may also discover it feels nice to touch the genital area. They cannot experience 'orgasm' as we know it – the activity is about the warm nice feelings they gain and not with the goal in mind that adults might have when we masturbate. The penis and clitoris are sensitive areas of the body, even for children. Remember, masturbation is not the sole domain of boys – girls masturbate as well. Thankfully, masturbation is no longer considered a mental illness and we no longer feel the need to chemically castrate young boys who participate in it or institutionalise and sterilise girls who do. These scenarios were still taking place in psychiatric hospitals as recently as the 1950s so our not too distant past has lots of messages about what was then called 'self-mutilation'. The Scout movement and production of cornflakes both came out of the desire to discourage 'youth' from this 'self-harming' activity.

Most people now accept it is a normal practice that does not harm the mental or emotional capacity of the child (or adolescent). It is, however, a private activity and just as we teach our children not to urinate or defecate in a public place, we need to point out that masturbation is done in private. This lesson therefore is about social mores rather than 'mortal sins'.

Some children will masturbate more often if they are feeling insecure, frightened, tired, and bored. If this activity seems to be preoccupying the child to the exclusion of other activities you may want to investigate just what is going on in their world and see if they are in need of some tender loving care. But that aside, they are not going to go blind or grow hairs on the palms of their hands just because they are masturbating.

As my mother pointed out to me, children raised in her generation usually didn't have their pants off for any length of time. Today we are far more likely to let our children run around naked or semi-naked and hence there is a lot more opportunity for the child to be aware of their genitals.

Nudity

Nudity can be fun. Many children and adults enjoy the freedom of having their clothes off and swimming in a river or running around in the bush. But unless you belong to a naturalist club, or have a very private backyard you are unlikely to indulge too often. The fact is that we have laws about public nudity for adults. There is also a social expectation that adults especially don't get their gear off in public, so you need to think about where and when it is appropriate for your child to be nude. Most people find it inoffensive to have one- to three-year-olds nude at the beach, but you may find it different if you try to take your child naked to the local public pool. There also comes a time at about four to five years when socially it seems okay for the child to have no top on but not okay for their penis or vagina to be exposed.

Take into account the environment you are in. Are there other children your child's age naked here? Is it going to be comfortable for other people if your child is nude? A mother told me recently that her six-year-old son had always been very comfortable to swim naked at the local beach. But one day they were there when some of his peers from school were also present and he became the butt of their jokes and ridicule. It is times like these when you start to realise that your relaxed and 'no worries' attitude may not be doing your child any favours in their own social development with their peer group.

Your child will develop their own sense of privacy from around four to five years of age and may start to tell you when they want clothes on or off – and when to keep yours on too! Listen to what they are telling you about their need for privacy. As amusing as it sometimes seems, it is important to them and it is about their personal physical boundaries. Encouraging and affirming this is a positive thing and allows them to know they are in charge of their own bodies – a very important message in the prevention of sexual abuse, and in determining their sexual behaviours in later life.

Bodies are beautiful, functional and amazing things – assisting your child to enjoy theirs and showing them that you enjoy, respect and honour your own and other people's bodies and boundaries is life-affirming.

4

Answering questions

Being an askable parent

As children grow and develop language they will start to ask all sorts of questions, some of which will be more challenging than others. It makes sense to answer them when they ask, and to tell the truth. If you are busy and can't answer right away, do make the effort to attend to it later. If you keep putting the child off by saying 'I'll tell you later', but actually don't, you eventually teach them you don't want to be asked those questions and they will stop asking you.

As discussed in previous chapters, some of the difficulty we as parents experience is based on our own understanding of sexuality issues and our own level of comfort with these. Children are seen as needing protection from so many dangers and sex almost always falls into the worst type of danger, thus so does knowledge about bodies, sexual parts of the body, conception and sexual behaviours.

I have friends who will let their primary-school-aged children watch hours of cartoons or videos that contain violence in many forms – however 'low level' – yet if these same programs contained 'low level' sex scenes those same parents would be grabbing the remote! Or some people will say that children wouldn't understand the sex scenes and would be confused by them – yet they supposedly understand violence.

Sex is seen as the ultimate thing that children need protection from – the ultimate destroyer of innocence.

We tend to panic therefore that if we answer all their questions about sex or sexuality they will somehow be violated or tainted by this knowledge. Try to shake off the response within yourself that these are 'dangerous' questions. Take a deep breath and simply remember that the child is curious and wants to know something. Being open and honest will not harm your child, but keeping secrets, having forbidden topics of conversation and fobbing off your child's questions about sexuality can lead to confusion, ignorance and feelings of shame about their gender, body and bodily functions.

Certainly within the last decade there has been an enormous change in the willingness of parents to talk to children about sexuality, but this is because of the growing awareness of sexual abuse. However abuse is only one aspect of sexual behaviour and it is a negative and painful aspect. We also need to acknowledge the positive aspects of human sexuality in order to give our children a balanced outlook.

A willingness to discuss the issues is the first step, becoming comfortable with the language and the facts is the second . . . and taking the leap into communication is the third. Being an askable parent is something that we need to practise from the beginning with our child and some of the ways we achieve this is simply by answering the many and varied questions that kids offer up to us every day.

'Why is the sky blue?' 'Does Jesus live in the sky with Superman?' 'Why do rabbits hop?' Being prepared to answer their questions as far as you can – even if you don't know all the answers – shows your child that you are approachable, will make time for them, do value them and do want to help them learn about their world.

If you are uncomfortable answering some questions, perhaps you can direct your child to your partner or a friend who you know will answer the question and who you have discussed these issues with previously.

Some parents become concerned that they may tell their children too much and that this can be harmful to the child. Some people may tell you that there is 'no need for them to know all that'.

'Since he was very young, Jack has particularly loved to hear the story of when he was "birthed". I tell him about me waking up and realising I was in labour, contractions, going to the hospital, how he came out my vagina, and so on. Because his best friend Isobel was born by Caesarean section, he has understood for a long time that some babies come out of their mother's tummies.'

Louise, mother of Jack

You only need to give as much information as you feel matches their level of understanding and that simply answers the question. On many topics your child may ask you again at a later date and need more complex information matching their developing ability to think and reason. This type of honesty is not a new concept, as the Reverend Kirsch's words from 1930 show. If you inform your child at their pace and as they grow, there really is no need for the 'big sex talk' in the puberty years, it becomes a redundant concept.

'Worse than ignoring the questions would be the practice of telling the child: "Children must not talk about such things". Such an answer would only stimulate his curiosity and drive him elsewhere for information or let him suspect that there is a mystery that the parents do not wish to discuss.'

– Rev. Felix Kirsch, 1930

Children only take in as much information as they need and are able to comprehend at the time.

If at age three they ask where babies come from, they are not seeking the whole procreation story of ovum and sperm, they are probably just asking if babies come from the sky, a cabbage patch or a hen's egg. It is quite sufficient to say 'from inside the woman's body in a place called the womb (uterus)'. If they want to know how the baby comes out, it's okay to tell them the truth.

Children will also revisit ideas over and over, taking in the information they need for now and adding to it over time, so just because you have told them once doesn't mean they won't ask again and again. They will also frame it in a way that they can understand, so even when you have given them careful, accurate information they may still retell it in a truly delightful concoction of reality and fantasy.

A time when children are very likely to ask questions is when they see pregnant women, or you yourself are expecting another child. It is all very exciting and intriguing for most children and they are curious to know how it all comes about.

By five years of age the child may well want more information about how the baby got into the woman's womb and you may feel comfortable to give a simplistic version of sex, such as 'Mummy and

'Alexandra asked me one day if women had to wear special underwear when they were pregnant, to make sure that the baby didn't fall out of their vagina when they walked around.'

Barbara, mother of two.

Daddy really loved each other and got very close, and one way to show their love was for Daddy to put his penis inside Mummy's vagina. After some days a baby started to grow inside Mummy's womb.'

How you describe the act of sexual intercourse will vary with each individual and you will no doubt place it in the context you are comfortable with. If you believe sex is only between people who love each other, or only between men and women, or only between married people, or that it is a pleasurable experience that can be shared by any two people who like each other, then say that. Be honest about the place of sex in your life and the lives of others. In today's world there are really no hard and fast rules for adults about who has sex with whom and when. Your own belief system and lifestyle will dictate what you tell your child. As children grow up they will be exposed to many variations on this theme, so start guiding them now in the beliefs that you hold as important.

Share only as much as you want to and feel is appropriate to their age and level of understanding. Children like to share their new knowledge, and some information you give them may be reinterpreted and shared out of its original context. You might find that at Playgroup your child shares with great excitement the news that 'Mum has sex with Tom because it's really good fun and they do it lots' – which is probably not how you intended the information to be used!

Telling your children about sexual intercourse is not harmful to them. Just because they hear about it does not mean that they will go out and do it. Indeed, research shows that if children grow up with an openness about sex and sexuality issues and they have their questions and concerns answered as they ask them, they are in fact more likely to delay their own first sexual encounters. So talking with your kids now is a good investment, allowing them to be wise about their sex choices in early adulthood. Educating them about the risks and pleasures of sex may be something you talk about as they enter their adolescent years – and let's face it, sex is meant to be pleasurable or most people wouldn't bother with it. You don't have to be Victorian about it and profess it's a duty or an unpleasant activity – they're going to wonder why on earth you do it if it's so awful!!

Sex is dirty
Save it for someone you love

Joani Blank

So what about morals? As parents we all seek to influence our children's behaviour and value system – that is after all what 'parental guidance' is all about.

Imparting a moral message becomes an implicit part of giving information; it is impossible to separate sexuality education from moral values. Just the words and manner in which you give the information to your child carries some moral tone and inference. So be assured the way you talk and the things that you do every day are all ways that you are imparting a moral message to your child – not all moral messages need to be spelt out in black and white. If you have decided that you really don't want to pass on your own inhibitions to your children then you are probably on the right track by reading this book and exploring where your values and discomfort came from. Making a conscious effort to give information rather than withhold it and to encourage your child's comfort with their body or gender rather than suppress it, are ways in which you counter the passing on of inhibitions.

Some parents worry that their children don't ask any questions at all about these issues and have shown no interest in sex or sexuality as they've grown. Maybe their children are simply absorbing that information as they go and don't feel the need to ask outright for information. If you have remained askable in other aspects of their life then it would seem senseless to start to worry because they don't ask about sex, or try to force the topic upon them. I think we've probably all heard the stories of young girls who have said to their enthusiastic mothers: 'Oh God, Mum, you're not going to tell me all about periods *again* are you?' Instead of forcing the issue, you may like to leave some books designed for kids on the bookshelf so that if and when they want to look at these they can, quietly and on their own. There is a list of good books for children on page 89.

What would you say if . . . ?

Here are some typical scenarios and suggestions for how you might deal with them. These are by no means the only responses to the situations and are merely a guide. An important aspect of any response is not to 'shame' the child by threatening them, exaggerating the consequences or lying. If you don't like what they are doing or saying you can let them know without implying that they are bad.

Your three-year-old sees a baby being breastfed and asks to suckle your breast.

You could say no, and explain that babies are fed by their mother's breast milk, but that when they grow older they learn how to drink out of cups and don't need to drink from the breast any more (and offer your child a cup of water/juice/milk instead). You might also explain that your breasts don't have any milk left now because it is only there while the baby is young.

You walk into a room and you see your three-year-old looking closely at the genitals of another child.

Acknowledge that they are obviously curious about penises and vaginas and offer to answer any questions they might have (be prepared to answer them however!) and then suggest that they play another game.

You are in the bath with your 2½ year old, who suddenly reaches out and touches your pubic hair/penis/vulva.

Move their hand gently away and acknowledge that yes, Mummy/Daddy has the same (or different) genitals as them, and explain that it's a private part of your body that you don't want other people to touch without your permission.

Your four-year-old starts to masturbate in the living room while watching television.

Talk to the child quietly and discover whether they are tired or bored. Tell them that what they are doing probably does feel nice for them, but that it is a private activity and that they should do it in their bedroom when alone.

While at a friend's house, your three-year-old takes their clothes off and starts running around the room laughing and having fun.

Tell them to put their clothes back on as it is not bathtime and no one else has their clothes off. Check whether they are bored, needing attention, too hot or just having fun.

Your preschooler asks the elderly neighbour if she has a penis or a vagina.

Explain to your child that Ms . . . probably won't want to answer that question, however all women have vaginas. Tell the child that it is not the sort of thing to ask people because it is about a private part of the body and it might embarrass them. (Then you can give your neighbour a resigned look that suggests 'Gee, don't kids ask the darnedest things!')

You are pushing your son around the supermarket and he starts to say in a loud voice 'Daddy/Mummy, my penis is sore'.

Acknowledge what they are telling you and assure them that you will attend to it as soon as you've finished in the supermarket (and do so).

Again at the supermarket and this time as you stroll past the shelves of tampons your child says loudly, 'Mummy you forgot to buy those things to stick up your bum when the blood comes out'.

Explain that Mum doesn't need them today, thank them for the reminder and that it would be nicer for Mum if they said it more quietly next time, because it is private for you. You might like to mention later that it's Mummy's vagina and not her bum that tampons go into.

Your preschooler gets upset because they see you changing a pad or tampon and they think you are injured.

Explain that once a month most women have blood coming out of their vagina. It is called their period and although it looks like lots of blood, it doesn't really hurt mummy, and it is not an injury. Explain that the tampon/pad stops the blood from messing up mum's panties, etc.

Your preschooler walks in on you and your partner engaging in sexual activity.

Stop what you are doing and ask them to please leave the room because you are having some private time. If they enquire later you may like to explain that what you were doing is a special private thing that grown ups do especially when they like/love each other, and that it is one way that grown ups show their liking/love for each other.

Your preschooler sees a pregnant woman when you are out shopping and asks 'why has that lady got such a fat tummy?'

Explain that the lady has a baby growing inside her tummy. That as the baby gets bigger so does the tummy and when the baby is fully grown it will come out. Of course you might get some more questions then about like 'how does it come out?' and it would be appropriate to tell your child that you will answer that and any other questions about it more when you get home.

Your four-year-old says that when he asked Jason why he had two mums, he said that it's because his mum is a lesbian. But your son wants to know what that means.

Explain that 'lesbian' is the word used to describe a woman who loves another woman. You could say: 'Just like I love your dad, well, Jason's mum loves her partner Julie'. Talk about how families are different, and some children have a mum and dad, two dads, or two mums, or maybe only one mum or dad. So instead of a dad Jason has an extra mum.

According to *Family Matters* (# 59), the journal of the Australian Institute of Family Studies, families headed by lesbian or gay parents are becoming more visible. In 1999, a NSW study found that of 386 lesbians surveyed, 22 per cent already had children and a further almost 20 per cent wanted them.

All of these responses have key things in common: acknowledging the child's behaviour, concerns, curiosity and feelings and then explaining why it may or may not be appropriate in this particular environment or situation. Try to answer the child or deal with the situation as it arises rather than simply avoiding the issue with a 'stop that' or an 'I'll tell you later'. Of course you might not realistically have the time right there and then, but if you say you'll tell them later, DO IT! Otherwise they'll remain ignorant, or seek the answer from someone else whose ideas you may not be at all comfortable with. And they learn that you are not an askable parent.

You may think that it is unnecessary to ask your child to speak softly in public about sexual issues, or to wear their clothes if they don't want to, etc., but the reality is that we do live within a society where there are codes of conduct. For your child to feel a part of and not apart from that society, they need to develop a knowledge of those codes during childhood. You are their most important teacher.

Talking about relationships

Relationships are a huge part of sexuality. And this is an aspect that perhaps we forget to give explicit information about – the reasons why Mum and Dad married, or have never married, or have separated/divorced. The reasons why adults don't always love each other 'forever'. The explanations about how we resolve conflict within our relationships, what loving someone is about, how we share and how we show people we care.

If we don't answer these types of questions too we are putting sexuality into the 'sex education' basket again and hence leaving out the vital components of how these issues and behaviours fit into our own lives – the human interaction aspects of sexuality. What is the code you want your child to live by? What is it that you want them to understand about being male or female and how sexual behaviours fit into that? There are plenty of teachable moments presented to us every day to discuss these broader aspects with our children, so look out for them. Television programs in particular present relationship or male–female interactions. The people within your system of family and friends also offer situations that may prompt a child's questions and present you with opportunities to answer these.

Shocking Grandma

So you've been busy being this amazing parent who works hard at openness and honesty with your children and who answers questions diligently, but when your child tells Grandma that Sally is having a baby because she had sex with Jim, Grandma goes nuts! I hasten to add that not all grandparents are by definition automatically 'old fashioned' or conservative. However you may discover that your parents or other relatives – and even your friends – may not see things the way you do when it comes to openness about sexuality and they may express shock or concern at the amount of detail or information you have imparted to your offspring.

'I was babysitting my three-year-old niece when she came in from the sandpit to tell me (with perfect enunciation), "Katie, I have sand in my vagina". I was a bit taken aback, but all I said was, "Well, into the bath you go!"'

Katie, auntie of Julia

Certainly some aging grandparents I have known have been perfectly at ease with the fact that many children now know and use the clinical terms for genitals and have knowledge about babies and birth that their own generation did not generally have. However these same people can be horrified to think that an eight-year-old child knows what the terms 'gay' or 'lesbian' mean – homosexuality being an aspect of sexuality that still remains taboo for them.

A lot of this resistance can be part of a strongly-held belief that the world has become too liberal and that children are doomed to be 'problem children' if they are allowed to ask too many questions – and gain answers.

Some older people are entirely mystified by the way many of us parent today anyway, let alone when we venture into the seedy world of sex and sexuality!

Sometimes you might just have to take a deep breath and let some of this stuff wash over you; it really depends on the type of relationship you have with the other adults concerned. If this is the mum and dad who told you that masturbation made people go blind or that only bad girls got heavy periods, then they may not have had any major rethinks on those issues in later life. But it is important to talk to your parents about how you do things, especially if your child sees a lot of them. If you don't feel able to talk about it with your parents or if they simply cannot see it your way, then you may want to spend some time explaining the differences in belief to your child as and if situations arise.

Your friends, and the parents of your child's friends, need consideration too. As close as you may be, you may still discover that here also lie some differences of opinion. If you want to avoid these issues driving a wedge between you, talking to your friends about how you are raising your child is a good idea.

> 'I had a call from a friend who had found my son and her daughter playing "doctors and nurses" at her house. She was really angry about it and felt that I should talk to him about good and bad touching, and that he was in the wrong, and so on. They were both four years old! She and I didn't speak about it for about three months afterwards.'
>
> *Claudia, mother of Josh*

The first time something like Claudia's experience happens can be a testing moment for a friendship. If you cannot agree on what is permissible behaviour, then see if you can at least agree on how to deal with the behaviour. A friend might tell you that they caught the kids 'at it' and redirected them to something else, and usually this is simply to keep you informed and keep the lines of communication open. Another time a friend may find it a very sensitive issue and become emotive in the way they bring it up. Simply telling your friend that you don't have a problem with what happened might not be enough. You may need to tell them that you understand and respect their point of view, but that you also need to reach some agreement about how you and they will deal with this if it comes up again. Sometimes it can swing in the other direction, with a friend saying airily: 'Oh, they always play those games at my house and I just leave them to it. It's harmless after all'. If this is contrary to your feelings, you may want to point out that while you accept that children are curious and do want to check things out, you would rather that they were redirected into another game. As in all things there is a middle ground, and while you and your friends may have different ideas of what this is, compromise is usually possible.

More than likely you and your friends have similar views on these issues but there can be some surprises from people you thought you knew well.

Remember, however, that sexuality is a very emotive issue. Your friends' views are valid and important to them and have been formed from their own lifetime of personal experiences, just as yours have.

5

Sexual
identity
and
orientation

What does it all mean?

In the 21st century it is almost impossible not to have heard the term 'sexual orientation', but what does all of this identity and orientation stuff really mean?

In the ground-breaking 'Kinsey Report', published in the USA in the 1940s, A.G. Kinsey's research found that an average of ten per cent of the population (thirteen per cent men, seven per cent women) was made up of people who had predominantly homosexual experiences. His study also indicated that a significant percentage of the population engaged in sexual activity with people of their own gender *at some stage of their life.*

As mentioned in earlier chapters it is quite common for young people to have sexual experiences with others of the same gender and that this does not necessarily mean that they are gay, lesbian or bisexual. Experimentation is a normal and natural part of childhood and adolescence.

I told David recently that one of his most beloved female adult friends had a girlfriend instead of a boyfriend. When they next visited, while I was inside preparing dinner and he was out in the garden he told my friend's partner he knew something secret about her – that she was our friend's girlfriend. I hadn't said that this was secret information or made a deal about it at all, so I was a little surprised.

Rachel, mother of a five-year-old

One current theory about sexual identity and orientation is the 'sexuality trichotomy model' (Kevin Haig & Tony Hughes, New Zealand Aids

Foundation, 1990) which states that there are three components to our sexuality. These are our sexual identity, our sexual orientation and our sexual behaviours. Our *sexual identity* is how we see ourselves and how we present ourselves to others; this could be as heterosexual, homosexual or bisexual. Our *sexual orientation* is something we do not control. This aspect of sexuality is predetermined, is unchangeable and is an integral part of our being. Sexual orientation is our physical, spiritual, sexual and emotional attraction to others. Finally, our *sexual behaviour* is what we do for sexual pleasure.

It is possible for one or more aspects of our sexuality to be in conflict. A simple example of this is a person who sees himself or herself as heterosexual and projects that image to the world, but who has sexual relationships with both men and women (bisexual behaviour) and has a homosexual sexual orientation; that is, an emotional and sexual attraction to the same sex. However the trichotomy model theorises that all three aspects of sexuality need to be integrated for the individual to be physically, spiritually, emotionally and sexually healthy.

Homophobia

Homophobia is the irrational fear of homosexuality, based on stereotypes. It is all the clichés about male nurses and hairdressers and female truckies with facial hair, and while it may seem like harmless joking, the impact of homophobia is perhaps best equated to racism. What this means for parents is that you need to be aware of the messages that you are passing on to your children, both implicitly and explicitly.

For example, it is erroneous to believe that homosexuality is the same as paedophilia (the vast majority of child sexual abusers are heterosexual in orientation).

One concern that parents may have is to wonder: 'Can I "turn" my child homosexual as a result of my parenting style?' Professional and popular opinion is divided as to whether homosexuality is due to genetic or environmental factors. And focusing on whether homosexuality or bisexuality comes about because of genetic or environmental factors is probably a red herring; what does matter is parental attitudes. A young girl who climbs trees, plays trucks, and likes her hair short or a young boy who plays with dolls and has a best friend who is a girl, may or may not 'come out' as gay or lesbian in later life. But your attitude now may influence your ability to talk to your children later on, irrespective of your child's sexuality.

> 'A parent's attitude will determine the child's ease of acceptance of (their own) sexuality and orientation, rather than have any influence on changing it.'
>
> *Kerry Price*

Negative reactions to harmless childhood behaviours can be damaging to the child's esteem. In most cases children are simply engaging in whatever games their peer group is playing as they grow and develop friendships. There are no guaranteed activities to engage in with your child to ensure they will be heterosexual, so why prohibit any activities based on supposed gender correctness?

The common fear about children 'becoming' gay or lesbian is usually borne out of the belief that this is not normal or acceptable, that it is somehow a defect in a child. Parents may also have concerns about how other people will treat the child as they grow into adulthood. Loving the child for who he or she is and engaging with them in games they enjoy are surely the most important considerations. That they grow up able to love and care about someone else is surely a sign of good parenting, regardless of whether the people they love are the same gender as themselves.

Parents' homophobic attitudes may affect a child's ability to communicate with them, affect their creativity and imagination, and may affect their behaviour (specifically in terms of bullying and social interactions), irrespective of their own orientation.

Embrace diversity. Teaching your child to value others, of different races, creeds, cultures, genders and orientations is a part of teaching them to embrace life and to value themselves alongside other people. Difference does not have to be feared.

This chapter co-authored with Kerry Price, Manager, Gay Men's Health Programs, New Zealand Aids Foundation

Some famous lesbian women

Queen Christina of Sweden (1626–1689)
Virginia Wolfe, writer
Eleanor Roosevelt, wife of US President Franklin
Roosevelt
Katherine Mansfield, writer
Sylvia Ashton Warner, writer
Bessie Smith, blues singer
Janis Joplin, singer
Dusty Springfield, singer
Martina Navratilova, international tennis player
Ellen DeGeneres, actor and comedian
Chastity Bono, daughter of Sonny and Cher
Linda and Jools Topp, actors, comedians and
singers
Rosie O'Donnell, talk show host
Melissa Etheridge, singer
k. d. lang, singer
Dr Kerryn Phelps, President, AMA
Julie McCrossin, comedian

Some famous gay men

Socrates, Greek philosopher

Alexander the Great, Greek ruler

Julius Caesar, Roman emperor

Richard the Lionheart, English king

Leonardo da Vinci, painter and inventor

Tchaikovsky, composer

Oscar Wilde, writer

Walt Whitman, writer

Sir Richard Burton, explorer

Rock Hudson, actor

Gianni Versace, designer

Nigel Hawthorne, actor

Richard Wherrett, theatre director

Freddie Mercury, singer

Julian Clary, comedian

Quentin Crisp, writer and actor

Elton John, singer

Rupert Everett, actor

Ian Roberts, Australian footballer

6

Sexual abuse

What is sexual abuse?

Sexual abuse is when a child is engaged by an adult in an act that is sexually arousing for the adult. It takes advantage of the power adults have over children and cannot involve consent because a child cannot consent. It may involve touching children sexually, getting them to touch an adult sexually, or making them watch sexual activity or pornographic videos, or look at other pornographic material.

Society is still coming to terms with the prevalence of abuse, and what we should do about addressing the issue. In the 1980s and early 1990s there were some national and international court cases that brought men as sexual abusers to the forefront of our minds. This has impacted on how vulnerable men feel in their role as parents and caregivers. This has all been an important part of a society coming to terms with the realities of abuse and hopefully our increased awareness will serve to provide a safer community as opposed to a fearful one.

Prevention

The predicament for parents is how do we teach children to view sex and sexuality positively, while at the same time warning them it can be used to harm them? In the previous chapters we have looked at how to give positive messages; here we need to acknowledge that some children may be exposed to hurtful sexual experiences.

The previous chapters have in fact been the groundwork and foundation for the prevention of sexual abuse. If we teach children from early in their lives about concepts of privacy, that their bodies are their own and that others should not touch their genitals without their permission, then we have already established some very important guidelines.

The globally-accepted figure is that one in four children will be sexually abused before the age of sixteen. While education about sexual abuse became popular during the 1980s, it was often skewed towards the 'stranger danger' concept. This is an erroneous approach as, although incidents involving 'strangers' are the ones that usually make the media headlines, statistics show that most abuse of children is by a family member or family friend and that the incidence of 'stranger' childhood sexual abuse is low in Australia and New Zealand. The stranger danger concept is one that perhaps your own parents taught you – this is the 'Don't take lollies or rides from strangers' rule, yet the truth is our parents weren't really talking about the lollies or the rides being dangerous.

In a way it is more comfortable for us to believe some trench coated stranger would do these awful things, than to acknowledge it is likely to be someone known to you and your child.

This by no means implies that strangers are 'safe' people to leave your children with, but the reality is that most child sexual abusers spend time 'grooming' the child and often the parents. By 'grooming' I mean that they gradually become trusted friends, liked by the child and perhaps by you.

Please don't become mistrustful of all the people you know, just use your common sense and don't leave your child in situations that would leave them open to opportunities for abuse. Go with your gut feelings and do listen to what your child tells you.

You may not always be able to protect your child from abuse, it may occur even with your very best efforts to keep them safe. What you can hope to have achieved is that your child knows they can talk to you about this, and that you will do something to protect them.

'When he was two and a half my young son was sexually abused by someone I trusted. When he returned from an outing with that person he told me that he didn't like them, that they were 'dumb' because they had played with his penis and other things. While I was devastated that this had happened to him, I was relieved that he had told me, and told me so immediately and it

meant I could do something straight
away to reassure him and to ensure that
person did not get near him again. I
still felt very sad though that I had
failed to protect him.'

Diane, mother of four

The concept of good and bad touching is one
way to talk about unwanted touch and can be introduced to the child when you talk about privacy and
private parts of the body. One way to explain the differences between touch you like and touch that
makes you feel fearful or 'yukky' is to compare this
to eating an ice cream which is nice or being forced
to eat tripe/stew which is not. Or the hug from a
parent that the child enjoys compared with being
pushed or hit by someone. You can then say that if
'yukky' touching happens they can tell the person
to stop or if they don't feel brave enough to do that,
they can tell you and you will listen to them and
help them.

If a child does tell you that something has happened to them it is very important that you listen,

thank them for telling you, reassure them it is not their fault, tell them you are sorry this has happened, and that you will help. They may have been told by the abuser not to tell, or that something awful will happen to them, you or a pet if they do tell, so the child may need lots of reassurance that nothing like that will happen.

The follow on effect of abuse in the form of loss of contact with a friend or family member can sometimes be devastating for the child, even when this person has abused them. Do seek advice and support from professionals if a situation of abuse does arise. Being abused can leave a child feeling disempowered and the actions you take afterwards can compound or ease these feelings (see 'Seeking help', p. 84).

Advice for fathers and other male carers

Statistically, sexual abusers are still more likely to be male than female (but women do abuse). This statistic and heightened community awareness has had some negative effects and resulted in a significant shift in how comfortable many fathers, stepfathers, grandfathers and carers such as teachers feel about physical contact with children. I have heard fathers talk about being fearful of having a bath with their children or taking their female child into a public toilet, in case it is seen as somehow deviant and inappropriate. This type of fear only serves to confuse child and parent and create situations where loving touch and playful intimacy do not take place for fear of accusations.

'As a single dad raising a girl I would feel really aware of this stuff sometimes. I remember travelling on a bus one day with my daughter when she was about five and she was sitting on my knee. People kept looking at us, and particularly at me, and I could tell they were suspicious, as if I was doing something abusive by having her on my knee. It was bloody awful, but I just had to think "to hell with them". It's sick.'

Luke, sole parent

Perhaps the yardstick for fathers and other male carers has to be that you surely know what is right or wrong in terms of appropriate contact with a child, just as Luke did in his experience (see box). If the same situation would not be inappropriate if a woman was involved, and if you have no intention of engaging the child in sexualised contact then it is *not* sexual abuse.

Seeking help

If your child is abused (or another child you know tells you they have been abused) you need to tell someone you trust and seek to reach some decisions about what to do next.

Protecting the child from the abuser is vital and you may need support in tackling this issue and also how you are feeling about what has happened.

Most major towns and cities will have HELP or Rape Crisis services. You can usually find these in the front of your telephone book under 'Community Help' in Australia and 'Personal Help Services' in New Zealand. These agencies can offer support to you as a parent and help you reach a decision about how you want to handle the situation. They will also offer you information about what can happen next, should you want to take this issue further. More contact numbers can be found on the next page.

In most Australian states and territories, professionals such as doctors are obliged by law to report cases they suspect could involve abuse to their community services department.

Although there is no legal obligation to report child sexual abuse in New Zealand, most health/ counselling professionals and government agencies are ethically bound to report abuse to the Child, Youth and Family Services (CYFS).

The CYFS is a government organisation that deals with (among other things) child disclosure of abuse as well as support for child and family should such a disclosure be made. This organisation may also involve the police in the process if criminal charges are to be laid. You may wish to contact CYFS for support and advice.

There is still debate about the usefulness of taking young children into counselling after sexual abuse, and often this will not take place unless the issues remain unresolved and arise for the child later on.

Useful Contacts

Australia
National NAPCAN Australia (National Association for Prevention of Child Abuse & Neglect): (02) 9211 0224
The NAPCAN website has a detailed, state-by-state help list, including reporting child abuse and support: www.napcan.org.au

State by state
Check the family/community services in your phonebook for more information

ACT	Family Services Northern Regional Office: (02) 6207 1069 Southern Regional Office: (02) 6207 1466 After hours: (02) 6207 0720
NSW	DoCs Helpline (free 24-hour child protection service): 132 111 Child Abuse Protection Services hotline: 1800 688 009
NT	24-hour NT-wide hotline: 1800 700 250
QLD	Families Youth & Community Care Brisbane metro: 07 3224 8045 Outside metro: 1800 811 810 After hours & emergency crisis care Brisbane metro: 07 3235 9999 Outside metro: 1800 177 135
SA	24-hour Child Abuse Report Line: 131 478
TAS	Child & Family Services: 1800 001 219
VIC	Child Protection Crisis Line (24 hours): 131 278
WA	Department for Community Development: (08) 9222 2555 1800 622 258 Police Child Abuse Unit: (08) 9492 5444
New Zealand	Department of Child, Youth and Family Services (national free call): 0508 326 459 Barnardo's family help line (national free call): 0800 222 345

Appendices

Books to read with your child

There are some good books that have been written for you to read with your child, or to make available to older children to read themselves. They should provide you and your child with some tender and fun-filled moments, where you both learn. If these books are not available from your bookshop, you will find a good selection in your local library or parenting centre.

Blank, Joani, *A Kid's First Book About Sex*, Yes Press, 1983
(For children aged five to ten years)
Chapouton, Ann-Marie, *A New Sister for Julian*, Dove Communications 1983

Cole, Joanna, *How You Were Born*, Morrow Junior Books, 1984

Cousins, Lucy, *Za Za's Baby Brother*, Walker Books, 1997

Hessell, Jenny, *Rebecca's Babies*, Century Hutchinson, 1988

Hessell, Jenny, *Staying at Sam's*, Collins, 1989
(Lovely book about the differences between families including comfort with nudity)

Hessell, Jenny, *What's Wrong with Bottoms*, Century Hutchinson, 1987
(Book to read with chidren about preventing sexual abuse)

Jackman, Wayne, *Our New Baby*, Firefly Books, 1990

Jones Sanchez, Gail with Gerbino, Mary, *Let's Talk about Sex and Loving*, Yes Press, 1983
(For children aged five to ten years)

Mayle, Peter, *Where Did I Come From?*, First Carol Publishing group, 1977

Stones, Rosemary, *Where Do Babies Come From?*, Puffin, 1989

Acknowledgments

I would like to thank the following people whose contributions have made this book possible:

Dr Ursula O'Sullivan for checking I had 'the facts' right, Kerry Price for his assistance with Chapter 5, John Boreham, Jo Stuthridge and Jon Marston for their encouragement and Marion Evans for first reading the manuscript. And also my thanks to those friends and parents who have shared their anecdotes with me over the years.

TODDLER TAMING
The guide to your child from one to four
Dr Christopher Green

More than a million parents all over the world swear by *Toddler Taming*, Dr Christopher Green's classic guide to surviving the toddler years. Now revised and updated for the twenty-first century, *Toddler Taming* offers friendly, practical advice for a whole new generation of parents.

Based on more than twenty years' experience, Dr Green's methods will help you to enjoy the toddler years. His reassuring message is to remember that you are normal and not alone.

DOUBLEDAY FAMILY ISSUES

BEYOND TODDLERDOM
Keeping five to twelve year olds on the rails
Dr Christopher Green

After surviving the toddler years, life with a five to twelve year old can seem like a roller-coaster ride of ups and downs, but with the help of the bestselling author of *Toddler Taming* you and your family will stay on the rails.

Beyond Toddlerdom is packed with practical, commonsense advice for parents of this 'in-between' age group. In his trademark warm and friendly style Dr Christopher Green shares his secrets for successful parenting and shows us how children think, feel and behave – and why.

DOUBLEDAY FAMILY ISSUES

THE KIDS AND US!
Eva Lewicki

A full-time job, two kids and a husband at home … the diary of a modern family.

A birthday party for a mob of eight-year-olds, house hunting with kids in tow and the teething problems of starting school. *The Kids and Us!* is for any parent who can see the funny side of parenting – or needs to. The 1.5 million people who read *That's Life!* magazine each week have followed the good times – and bad – of Eva Lewicki, her househusband Jules and young children Sophie and Alex, for four years. You'll laugh, you'll cry and you'll end up loving this fly-by-the-seat-of-her-pants domestic diary.

Eva Lewicki's column 'The Kids and Us!' has a phenomenal following among readers of *That's Life!* magazine. Eva works full-time as a journalist while juggling a demanding life with her harassed husband, energetic children and various pets including six Sea Monkeys, a rabbit, a hen, fifteen fish and a cat.

BANTAM BOOKS